Critical
Thinkers

Critical Thinkers

G. JANICE MILLER

ARPress
ILLUMINATING IDEAS.
EMPOWERING VOICES

ARPress
45 Dan Road Suite 5
Canton MA 02021

Hotline: 1(888) 821-0229
Fax: 1(508) 545-7580

Ordering Information:
Quantity sales. Special discounts are available on quantity purchases by corporations, associations, and others. For details, contact the publisher at the address above.

Printed in the United States of America.

ISBN-13:	Softcover	979-8-89389-370-0
	Hardcover	979-8-89389-371-7
	eBook	979-8-89389-369-4

Library of Congress Control Number: 2024916670

Contents

Introduction

Who has time for critical thinking? We have work to do! That statement is like starting on a long trip with an empty gas tank; but deciding you don't have time to stop and fuel-up.

Critical thinkers turn over all the rocks and go where the information leads. They defeat human tendencies to think in fragments which can lead to deception and the delusional mindset that Paul described in 2 Thessalonians 2:10. As we'll discuss later in the book, critical thinking has little to do with a person's IQ; but everything to do with their mindset.

What is the current state of critical thinking? Paul Hurd said, "Too many facts, too little conceptualizing; too much memorizing, and too little thinking." For over 30 years, one of the highest-level concerns among world leaders has been the deficiency in quality thinking skills. It is common to see article titles such as: "The Emerging Crisis in Critical Thinking," PsychologyToday.com, March 21, 2017.

The Foundation for Critical Thinking says that studies demonstrate most college faculty lack a substantive concept of critical thinking. However, most don't realize they lack. They believe they have a substantial understanding and assume they are teaching it to students.

What is critical thinking? The Foundation's definition is:

The capacity to evaluate skillfully and fairly the quality of evidence and detect error, hypocrisy, manipulation, dissembling (concealing one's true motives), and bias.

A critical thinker does not say, "My thinking is just fine. If everyone thought like me, this would be a pretty good world."

A critical thinker says, "My thinking, as that of everyone else, can always be improved. Self-deception and folly exist at every level of human life. It is foolish to ever take thinking for granted.

To think well, we must regularly analyze, assess, and reconstruct thinking – ever mindful as to how we can improve it."

Satan loves fragmented, shallow thinking. Fragmentation, according to Dictionary.com, is the process or state of breaking into small or separate parts, disintegration, collapse, and the breakdown of norms of thought, behavior, or social relationship.

Substantive knowledge is found in a set of fundamental and powerful concepts and principles that lie at the heart of understanding everything else in a discipline or subject. Fragmented, shallow thinking is an enemy of Ephesians 4:13 KJV where Paul said, "Till we all come in the unity of the faith, and of the knowledge of the Son of God, unto a perfect man, unto the measure of the stature of the fullness of Christ."

We live in a culture where we are encouraged to form and vocalize opinions and judgments before we have an adequate foundation to understand the topic. Couple this with the human tendency to overestimate our scope of understanding and it results in perpetuating fragmentation. We tend to train our minds to think in sound bites and 280-character tweets.

In Jesus' Parable of the Sower (Luke 8:4-15), three of the four people that were recipients of the seeds were fragmented. Only one of the four had a foundation to receive and process the seeds. In Jesus' Parable of the Two Builders (Matthew 7:24-27), He teaches the importance of the foundation we build on; a foundation that the enemy cannot penetrate. When we see the outcome of these two parables, we can see why Satan loves our shallow, fragmented thinking. It leads to collapse and makes his job easy.

God is calling us today to wake up and see what the enemy of our souls is doing. We must be sober and diligent. Paul admonishes us in Ephesians 6:10 KJV, "Finally, my brethren, be strong in the Lord, and in the power of His might." We need a solid foundation that the enemy cannot penetrate. We must be aware of the tactics of our enemy.

Chapter 1

What do Critical Thinkers do differently?

Spirit-led critical thinkers have a pure mindset and heart that distinguish them. Being a Spirit-led critical thinker has less to do with a person's IQ; but everything to do with an unhindered relationship with God. Unhindered meaning free from self; biases and entrapments and a clear understanding between the weightier matters versus those that are inconsequential.

A spiritual mind is completely open to God's Word and His Spirit; allows Him to control their thoughts, actions and motives and dismantle anything in their lives that prevent shaping them into the image of Christ. Other characteristics of Spirit-led critical thinkers:

- They have a clear vision of rational decision making because they use the Word of God to examine and evaluate their reasoning processes;
- They understand the pitfalls to which all human reasoning is subject because of uncritical and biased thought patterns that form dangerous ruts in their mental filters;
- They practice critical thinking so their mental filters are shaped according to the Word of God; resulting in whole thinking.

Making a list of some of the Biblical servants we can describe as Spirit-Led Critical Thinkers might include names like: Daniel, the Three Hebrew Children, Nehemiah, Esther, Moses, Isaiah, Jeremiah, Habakkuk, Bezalel, Paul, John the Revelator and many more.

When Daniel and the Three Hebrew children were identified to serve in King Nebuchadnezzar's court the qualifications the king was looking for included:

- No blemishes
- Well favored
- Skillful in all wisdom
- Endued with knowledge
- Skillful in science
- Ability to stand in the king's palace
- Capable of teaching the literature and language of the Chaldeans

We certainly recognize the importance of Daniel and the Three Hebrew Children meeting the king's qualifications because God had a purpose for their lives in the king's court and jurisdiction. However, more importantly, they met God's higher qualifications long before King Nebuchadnezzar was in the picture. In the midst of a people given to idol worship, and religious syncretism where they worshipped both God and idols, Daniel and his companions were righteous and had not bowed to an idol. They were completely committed to God and His will, unencumbered with the things around them. They didn't have any self-interests or lusts to protect. They were totally yielded as instruments of God for whatever He needed from them.

Because they knew their God, the Three Hebrew Children saw the bigger picture and kept their wits when faced with the fiery furnace (Daniel 3). The Son of God joined them in the furnace that day and the TRUTH prevailed. Daniel 11:32 KJV states, "…but the people that do know their God shall be strong and do exploits." Why? Because they are not unstable and double-minded. They have a pure heart and mind and have nothing to hide. They have pure faith because they are unencumbered. There is boldness of God's Spirit that rises up within them to do spiritual warfare "through God to the pulling down of strong holds…and every high thing that exalteth itself against the knowledge of God." 2 Corinthians 10:4-5 KJV.

Critical thinking, according to Professor Michael B. Metzer, Indiana University, is allowing our ideas, beliefs, and intuitions to be subject to systematic scrutiny. Critical thinkers want to know where their information is coming from, whether it is accurate, relevant, and adequate to the task at hand. We must know we are interpreting information correctly because we can make accurate information useless by interpreting it incorrectly. Critical thinking is hard work and takes on the tough, and many times painful, issues.

Professor Metzer describes the three categories of questions that critical thinkers understand and use:

1. *Opinion* questions – where there are a lot of "right" answers. For example: what is your favorite color, flavor, football team or brand of sneakers?
2. *Knowledge* questions – where there is only one "right" answer. For example: what side of the ledger does a debit go on? How much is two plus two? At what temperature does water boil at this altitude?
3. *Judgment* questions – where there are a number of possible answers, some of which may be better than others. For example: How should an economy be run? What should the maximum marginal tax rate be? Is debt ok? Should one invest in the stock market?

Critical thinkers have a clear understanding that the foundation they build in the *knowledge* category determines their effectiveness in the *judgment* and *opinion* categories. They know that until they have a strong knowledge foundation, it is reckless to form judgments and opinions. Thinking is hard work, and we are not naturally inclined to turn over all the rocks. That's why critical thinkers are in short supply in our world. Sometimes it's painful because it may be revealing things about ourselves we do not want to delve into. This may cause some to say that ignorance is bliss. But we must ask ourselves if the bliss is purchased at too high a price.

Let us consider the mindset of a person who completes 6 years of elementary school (grades 1 through 6) versus someone (equally as competent as person 1) who chooses to repeat the first grade 6 times because it doesn't require a challenge. They've both logged 6 years in school; but there's a vast difference. Many Christians are content to remain indefinitely in first grade, spiritually. This isn't new. The writer of Hebrews addressed it in his day. "For though by this time you ought to be teachers, you need someone to teach you again the basic principles of the oracles of God. You need milk, not solid food, for everyone who lives on milk is unskilled in the word of righteousness, since he is a child. But solid food is for the mature, for those who have their powers of discernment trained by constant practice to distinguish good from evil. Hebrews 5:12-14. Discernment is the highest form of knowledge because it has been revealed by God.

We typically bristle at the suggestion that our own reasoning processes may be biased. What? You are saying that I'm not completely rational and objective? That can't be true. Professor Metzer discusses several human tendencies that affect the quality of our thinking; forming ruts that filter how we see everything:

- Belief Bias – Ronald Kellogg, in his book, Cognitive Psychology, stated people tend to accept any and all conclusions that happen to fit with their systems of belief.
- Confirmation Bias – people are predisposed to believe things that are consistent with their pre-existing beliefs and to disbelieve things that contradict them. They are also strongly predisposed against seeking out information that would contradict their opinions.
- Overconfidence Bias – people tend to have an excessive confidence in their judgments and opinions. J. Edward Russo and Paul Schoemaker wrote an article titled, "Managing Overconfidence," in which they state good decision making requires more than knowledge of facts, concepts, and relationships. It also requires metaknowledge which is an understanding of the limits of our knowledge. Some of the most challenging individuals we will ever encounter are those who don't know what they don't know. They assume what they know about something is all there is to know.
- Denial – the tendency to discount or ignore unwelcome information.
- Excuses – The French author, Albert Camus said, "Each of us insists on being innocent at all costs, even if he has to accuse the whole human race and heaven itself."

- Positive Illusions/Self-Serving Biases – the tendency for our egos to tell us we are superior humans without seeing any weaknesses. Paul admonished us in Romans 12:3, "For by the grace given to me I say to everyone among you not to think of himself more highly than he ought to think, but to think with sober judgment, each according to the measure of faith that God has assigned."

In contrast to critical thinking, shallow thinking is concerned only with the surface. Satan takes advantage of shallow thinking to promote his agenda. He is always looking for people who are willing to sell their brains. Eve was willing to sell her brain to the serpent (aka Satan) and allow him to do her thinking. She was dealing with the lust for power and independence, and the serpent just happened to be running a special that day in the Garden. Instead of asking probing questions and analyzing the situation, she took him at his word. He did not have the power to make promises to her; but she didn't conclude that. His words were nothing more than air. If she had been wanting to find truth she would have put the conversation with the serpent on hold while she had a discussion with God about this situation. But her lust drove her to seek immediate satisfaction. Satan counts on that from humans.

American fraudster, Bernie Madoff, is currently serving a 150-year prison sentence for running an elaborate Ponzi scheme where many rich and famous people sold their brains. He was promising greater wealth; but it was built on air, not substance.

Cult leader, Jim Jones, led more than 900 followers in a mass suicide known as the Jonestown Massacre. He promised these people utopia if they would follow him. Had they not sold their brains to him they would have been able to reason that he did not have the power to give utopia.

Satan's entire network is built on emptiness. No substance; just air. But he is an expert at illusions. He paints beautiful pictures that make people willing to sell their brains because they are looking for immediate satisfaction for their lust(s).

In contrast, God has all power to fulfill His Word. There's no emptiness with Him; it's ALL substance. He welcomes us to taste and see that He is good. He doesn't ask us to sell our brain because He has nothing to hide. 1 Peter 2:22 states that Jesus committed no sin and there was no deceit found in His mouth. The more we learn of Him the more we stand in awe of His greatness and His majesty. He is truth! Paul writes in Romans the 4th chapter about Abraham's experience of walking with God. He knew God had the power to do what He had promised.

Is it a Christian's responsibility to cultivate critical thinking in themselves and others? Where do emotions fit in? What does it all mean in light of the greatest commandment?

Spirit-led critical thinkers understand that the Word of God is TRUTH; and is the basis for all truth. They comprehend the differences between opinion, knowledge and judgment; and the boundaries for opinion and judgment. For example: If we esteem our opinion above truth we are in a dangerous place; but many are comfortable doing so.

Why is it so important to embrace truth? Paul, teaching about end-times, describes a people in 2 Thessalonians 2:10-12 ESV, "and with all wicked deception for those who are perishing, because they refused to love the truth and so be saved. Therefore, God sends them a strong delusion, so that they may believe what is false, in order that all may be condemned who did not believe the truth but had pleasure in unrighteousness." A delusion is a belief or altered reality that is persistently held despite evidence or agreement to the contrary. It is no small matter to choose our opinions over truth. This indifference to truth is unrighteousness and without repentance we will travel down the road that Paul is describing. We can't treat this casually; but must understand the weight of this matter.

From day one of our Christian walk as we search the Scriptures and allow God's Spirit to reveal things in our lives that are not like Him, we are presented with a choice. We either allow Christ to shape us; or we decide to stand still, become stagnant, and not go any further in our walk. Those that choose to continue walking daily are on an upward spiral where they *learn* (revelation from the Word); *commit* (dedication to continue walking in personal relationship with Christ) and *do* (carry out Christ's instructions).

Chapter 2
The Spiritual Selfie

Seeing ourselves and our actions fairly and honestly is a valuable thing to have because it's so rarely attained. Introspection (soul-searching, self-examination) is so necessary to having a proper foundation that Jesus taught it in His Sermon on the Mount. In short, Jesus declared that being effective with others starts by looking in the mirror.

> ³Why do you see the speck that is in your brother's eye, but do not notice the log that is in your own eye? 4 Or how can you say to your brother, 'Let me take the speck out of your eye,' when there is the log in your own eye? 5 You hypocrite, first take the log out of your own eye, and then you will see clearly to take the speck out of your brother's eye. Matthew 7:3-5 ESV

Charles C. Manz wrote in *The Leadership Wisdom of Jesus*, "We can be blinded by the gratifying feeling of power over others that enables us to forget how flawed, how messed up we ourselves are." The less objective we are with ourselves, the less likely we are to be aware of it. Psychologist Jean Piaget said, "The less a mind is given to introspection, the more it is the victim of the illusion that it knows itself thoroughly."

An article in the May 12, 2017 Wall Street Journal, titled, "Why Golfers Overestimate Their Ability," helps us understand the importance of making decisions based on accurate data. The reporter, Brian Costa, wrote, "New data shows that golfers of all abilities think they will hit the ball farther than they do." The interesting part of the article isn't golfing statistics, but rather a theme that pertains to not only golfers, but all humans. The writer describes it as, "the persistent—and tough to overcome—cognitive bias that causes many players to regularly choose the wrong club." In other words, the golfers are surprised when the ball doesn't reach the mark; but, in reality the wrong club was used based on incorrect data (an inflated view of one's ability to hit the ball). Mr. Costa quoted David Dunning, a psychology professor at the University of Michigan, "The tendency reflected in the Arccos data is consistent with a phenomenon I have studied for two decades: why people overestimate their ability."

Paul said, "For by the grace given me I say to every one of you: Do not think of yourself more highly than you ought, but rather think of yourself with sober judgment, in accordance with the faith God has distributed to each of you." Romans 12:3 NIV.

When we make decisions based on inaccurate data, we miss the mark. What is the cure? Walking humbly before God. Humility is living in a state where we have a clear view (accurate data) of who God is and who we are. Walking in humility cures the sin of the bias of thinking too highly of ourselves. Our sufficiency is of God; not ourselves.

8He has shown you, O mortal, what is good. And what does the LORD require of you? To act justly and to love mercy and to walk humbly with your God. Micah 6:8 NIV.

Shallow thinking can take us down a path of idolatry without us realizing it. If a complete stranger were to observe my actions and listen to my conversations for 24 hours with no other information available, what would they conclude concerning who or what I worship?

Idolatry is idolization, adulation, adoration, glorification, hero-worship, and extreme admiration, love and reverence for someone/something other than God.

Even with all God's admonitions to His children, Israel, concerning not worshipping other gods; they chose to do it anyway. There was a common thread woven through the mainstream "other god" worship of that day: it was appealing to "the flesh." Satan devised a slick plan, presented it to God's people; and they bought it. What was the plan? An option where they could put a check mark in the "worship" box while allowing "the flesh" to remain alive and well. Satan still presents that same plan today - to saint and sinner alike. In contrast, The Father's plan is described by Jesus in Matthew 16:24 KJV, "Then said Jesus unto his disciples, if any man will come after Me, let him deny himself, and take up his cross, and follow Me." The flesh cannot be a survivor in Jesus' plan.

So, what happens if one wants the benefits of being on God's plan, but prefers not to deny self? Some people attempt to use workarounds. King Ahaz of Judah attempted one of the most egregious workarounds in history. II Chron 28:2 KJV, "For he walked in the ways of the kings of Israel and made also molten images for Baalim." II Chron 28:23, "For he sacrificed unto the gods of Damascus, which smote him: and he said, Because the gods of the kings of Syria help them, therefore will I sacrifice to them, that they may help me. But they were the ruin of him, and all Israel." Ahaz wanted to engage the gods of Syria for help since Syria, in his eyes, was enjoying success. Ahaz failed to realize that the gods of this world bring nothingness.

If we're putting a check mark in the worship box but we're entangled with "other god" worship (lust for power, the love of money, self-exaltation, self-preservation, self-serving biases...); then we've bought into the same plan as Israel - just a different century.

Jesus taught us the remedy for the sin of idolatry:

> [35]Then one of them, which was a lawyer, asked Him a question, tempting Him, and saying, [36]Master, which is the great commandment in the law? [37]Jesus said unto him, Thou shalt love the LORD thy God with all thy heart, and with all thy soul, and with all thy mind. 38This is the first and great commandment. [39]And the second is like unto it, Thou shalt love thy neighbour as thyself. [40]On these two commandments hang all the law and the prophets. Matthew 22:35-40 KJV.

Isaiah allowed us to observe his time of crisis and introspection:

> "In the year that King Uzziah died, I saw the Lord sitting upon a throne, high and lifted up; and the train of his robe filled the temple. Above him stood the seraphim. Each had six wings: with two he covered his face, and with two he covered his feet, and

with two he flew. And one called to another and said: Holy, holy, holy is the Lord of hosts; the whole earth is full of his glory! And the foundations of the thresholds shook at the voice of him who called, and the house was filled with smoke. And I said: "Woe is me! For I am lost; for I am a man of unclean lips, and I dwell in the midst of a people of unclean lips; for my eyes have seen the King, the Lord of hosts!" Isaiah 6:1-5 ESV.

God gives each of us a choice: we can dwell in the shallow or we can look up to the King of Kings. For those who choose to look up, we see ourselves in the light of God's glory, and we tend to be silent in His presence; because we see how destitute we are on our own.

Chapter 3
Eve's Speaking Tour: Beware of Deception

If Eve were on a speaking tour today, perhaps her main topic would be a warning about the power of deceit; which, if believed, results in us putting our faith in what is false. No doubt her message would be very compelling because it would be based on her true story.

Giving false or inaccurate information deliberately intended to deceive has been around since *before* Adam and Eve. Lucifer (aka Satan) gave out disinformation in Heaven and managed to deceive 1/3rd of the angels into following him.

Satan deputized and organized his staff of fallen angels to roam the earth and spread lies; starting with Adam and Eve in the Garden and Continuing today.

When we say that Satan wants to be worshipped instead of God, there's more to the story than he is narcissistic and wants to be the center of attention. He actually wants to be the **determiner of truth**.

> [7]And there was war in heaven: Michael and his angels fought against the dragon; and the dragon fought and his angels, [8]And prevailed not; neither was their place found any more in heaven. [9]And the great dragon was cast out, that old serpent, called the Devil, and Satan, which deceiveth the whole world: he was cast out into the earth, and his angels were cast out with him. Revelation 12:7-9.KJV
>
> "How you are fallen from heaven, O Day Star, son of Dawn! How you are cut down to the ground, you who laid the nations low! [13]You said in your heart, 'I will ascend to heaven; above the stars of God I will set my throne on high; I will sit on the mount of assembly in the far reaches of the north;[a] [14]I will ascend above the heights of the clouds; I will make myself like the Most High.' Isaiah 14:12-14 ESV

Ezekiel 28:12-18 describes the scene in Heaven when iniquity was found in Lucifer. He was intoxicated with pride to the point that he stepped outside the bounds of his authority as an angel. His reasoning became so sloppy he thought he could rise up and challenge God's authority. He wants his corrupt way to become *the* way. In his delusional mind, he *is* on the throne. Why do people keep falling for it? Because it speaks to a lust they are holding on to. James 1:14 KJV, "But every man is tempted, when he is drawn away of his own lust, and enticed." It isn't that people are standing back looking at the big picture and deliberately saying they are going to follow Satan rather than God; but instead, they are looking for an immediate fix for their lust. There's no thinking involved. It's like an animal that follows its instincts without the ability to think or reason. What people don't see at the outset is that on the other end of the stick and carrot, (that promises to scratch the itching lust), there's Satan pulling the stick into his delusional throne room. God created humans to be better than this. He created us with the capacity to think and reason and learn.

God's Word is TRUTH. "Sanctify them through thy truth: thy word is truth." John 17:17 KJV. His word will last forever. "The grass withers, the flower fades, but the word of our God will stand forever." Isaiah 40:8 ESV. The Word teaches us about Satan's deception toolbox; our human lusts that drive us to be deceived; and God's remedy.

We must realize that Satan's plan isn't complicated. He has maintained the same plan throughout history; probably because it keeps working on humans who decide studying God's Word, praying and critical thinking are hard work and they prefer to opt out. Here's his plan:

1. <u>First, Satan attempts to corrupt the Word of God.</u>
   The serpent told Eve in the Garden: "Ye shall not surely die." Genesis 3:4 KJV. This is opposite of God had told Adam recorded in Genesis 2:17.

   This practice of trying to corrupt the Word of God has continued throughout history. God had a conversation with Jeremiah about the issue in his day.

   [14] And the LORD said to me: "The prophets are prophesying lies in My name. I did not send them, nor did I command them or speak to them. They are prophesying to you a

lying vision, worthless divination, and the deceit of their own minds. [15]Therefore, thus says the LORD concerning the prophets who prophesy in my name although I did not send them, and who say, "Sword and famine shall not come upon this land." By sword and famine those prophets shall be consumed. [16]And the people to whom they prophesy shall be cast out in the streets of Jerusalem, victims of famine and sword, with none to bury them—them, their wives, their sons, and their daughters. For I will pour out their evil upon them." Jeremiah 14:14-16 ESV

Paul admonished his mentee, Titus, the need to be diligent in the sound teaching of God's Word because there were many insubordinates who were empty talkers; deceivers who were upsetting people and teaching what they shouldn't teach. And they were doing it for sordid (dishonorable, unworthy) gain.

[9]He must hold firm to the trustworthy word as taught, so that he may be able to give instruction in sound[a] doctrine, and also to rebuke those who contradict it.

[10]For there are many who are insubordinate, empty talkers and deceivers, especially those of the circumcision party.[b] [11]They must be silenced, since they are upsetting whole families by teaching for shameful gain what they ought not to teach. Titus 1:9-11 ESV

To his mentee, Timothy, Paul admonished him to become skillful in the Word so he could rightly handle the Word of Truth.

[15]Do your best to present yourself to God as one approved,[a] a worker who has no need to be ashamed, rightly handling the word of truth. 2 Timothy 2:15 ESV

Some manipulate or mishandle Scripture to support their personal agenda. It's called "proof-texting" and occurs when someone has a point they want to prove. They find a verse that supports their position even if it means stretching or ignoring the context in which the verse is found.

To minimize the possibility of misusing Scripture, it behooves us to: study the Word consistently (in a fair and impartial way) and continually (regularly, without interruption); pray for discernment; research before speaking; pursue righteousness; do justly; love kindness and walk humbly.

Paul told the Ephesians that all things become visible when they are exposed by the light. Ephesians 5:13. Satan hates the Word of God because it exposes who he is and what he does.

The Word of God has the power to discern our motives.

> [12]For the word of God is living and active, sharper than any two-edged sword, piercing to the division of soul and of spirit, of joints and of marrow, and discerning the thoughts and intentions of the heart. Hebrews 4:12 ESV

The Word of God discerned the true motives of Judas. He didn't care about the poor, he just wanted to put his hands on the money because he was a thief.

> [1]Six days before the Passover, Jesus therefore came to Bethany, where Lazarus was, whom Jesus had raised from the dead. [2]So they gave a dinner for him there. Martha served, and Lazarus was one of those reclining with him at table. [3]Mary therefore took a pound[a] of expensive ointment made from pure nard, and anointed the feet of Jesus and wiped his feet with her hair. The house was filled with the fragrance of the perfume. [4]But Judas Iscariot, one of his disciples (he who was about to betray him), said, [5]"Why was this ointment not sold for three hundred denarii[b] and given to the poor?" [6]He said this, not because he cared about the poor, but because he was a thief, and having charge of the moneybag he used to help himself to what was put into it. John 12:1-6 ESV

In John the 8th chapter we get a clear view of people who have succumbed to the flesh, but they are still trying to wear the religious label. The account is recorded in verses 12 – 51. Jesus has just stated to the crowd, "I am the light of the world: he that followeth me shall not walk in darkness, but shall have the light of life." Satan hates truth. When Jesus spoke that He is the light of the world, Satan couldn't tolerate those words. He had to retaliate. Unfortunately, the Pharisees (the religious ones) were willing instruments to help the evil one. It was because of their lust for power and control that they were willing to yield themselves as servants of Satan to work against the Truth. They should have recognized who Jesus was, but their sins blinded them. As soon as Jesus declared He is the light of the world, the Pharisees took a classic move out of Satan's deception handbook. They called Jesus a liar. They tried to paint an illusion for all the observers. Jesus did not back down. He told them they didn't understand His words because they have a different father—the devil (verse 44). Jesus told them their father is a liar and the father of all lies. That's why they didn't believe Him.

If we are in a similar situation today, do we know the Word and walk in the Spirit to discern the truth; or, because of own lusts, we find ourselves falling for moves out of Satan's deception handbook?

When we do not study the Word consistently and continually and pray for discernment, we leave ourselves vulnerable to deceit. Conversely, when we deny self and follow Christ into the depts of God's Word and Spirit, we take on a boldness in Him and we're able to see through His eyes rather than our own.

A. W. Tozer wrote, "If good men were all for union and bad men for division, or vice versa, that would simplify things for us. Or if it could be shown that God always unites and the devil always divides, it would be easy to find our way around in this confused and confusing world. But that is not how things are...In a fallen world like ours, unity is no treasure to be purchased at the price of compromise. Loyalty to God, faithfulness to truth, and the preservation of a good conscience are jewels more precious than the gold of Ophir or diamonds from the mine. For these jewels men have suffered the loss of property, imprisonment, and even death...."

Job said, "I have not departed from the command of His lips; I have treasured the words of His mouth more than my necessary food." Job 23:12 NASB.

"The secret of the Lord is with them that fear Him; and He will shew them His covenant." Psalm 25:14 KJV. Jesus is calling His children to move from the shallow surface into the depths of His truth. It will change how we see things. Pursuing righteousness will become more important to us than winning.

The highest level of understanding and knowledge a human can experience in this life is spiritual discernment. It goes beyond what is possible for a person to know on their own. It's spiritual; not natural. The Spirit illuminates the Word as we take each step and reveals to us the things only known by God. Paul said, "But God hath revealed them unto us by His Spirit: for the Spirit searcheth all things, yea, the deep things of God." 1 Corinthians 2:10 KJV. "But the natural man receiveth not the things of the Spirit of God: for they are foolishness unto Him: neither can He know them, because they are spiritually discerned." 1 Corinthians 2:14 KJV. This involves a level of trust that isn't natural to humans. It is developed in committed relationship with Christ. Each day is a learning experience as the Spirit reveals what we need for the step we are on.

A person walking in discernment knows that God is the owner of all knowledge and understanding; and He reveals it according to His will as we walk humbly before Him. Those that walk in the flesh feel that they own knowledge and understanding and even take liberty to use Scripture out of context.

1. Second, Satan paints illusions to satisfy human lusts.
   1 John 2:15-16 gives us the three categories of sins known to man. Every sin committed is preceded by at least one of these temptations:

   a. Lust of the Flesh – the temptation to feel physical pleasure from some sinful activity – to make the flesh feel satisfied. Paul gave us examples of the "works of the flesh" in Galatians 5:19-21 ESV, "Now the works of the flesh are evident: sexual immorality, impurity, sensuality, idolatry, sorcery, enmity, strife, jealousy, fits of anger, rivalries, dissensions, divisions, envy, drunkenness, orgies, and things like these. I warn you, as I warned you before, that those who do such things will not inherit the kingdom of God."

   b. Lust of the Eyes – things that appeal to the ego for self-gratification and self-promotion. Coveting.

   c. Pride of Life – anything that exalts us above our station and offers the illusion of God-like qualities; wherein we boast in arrogance and worldly wisdom.

If we were writing an article to describe how Satan's plan affects us, it could read:

Garage Sale: Priceless Art Being Sold for Pennies

On Oct 23, 2009, ABC News reported an original Picasso painting worth millions was sold for $2 at a garage sale. When the lady, who sold the piece, later found out its worth she said, "I had no idea in my wildest dreams. I was told it wasn't real and not to worry about it." She stated the obvious. Of course, she didn't know; otherwise her actions would have been different. She allowed someone, without researching for herself, to reprice a painting worth millions down to $2. She fell for it.

Here are a few examples of other garage sale finds:
$10,000 painting sold for 50 cents
$25,000 mirror sold for $2
$25,000 record sold for 75 cents
$43,000 Vince Lombardi sweater sold for 58 cents
$477,650 Declaration of Independence copy sold for $2.48
$541,500 table sold for $25
$2 million Andy Warhol sketch sold for $5
$2.2 million ceramic bowl sold for $3
And, one of the most notable in history: Esau sold his birthright for a bowl of stew.

God is the One who placed the value on our souls. He determined the value to be worth His Son's life; the highest value possible. However, He gave us the choice to reprice our soul or to give someone/something else the power to reprice as we see fit. But allow me to state the obvious. For us to reprice is equivalent to selling priceless art for pennies. Eve allowed the serpent to reprice for her and Adam and we know how that turned out.

Who/what are you allowing to reprice your soul?

John tells us (John 1:10-11) that Christ came into the world that He had made, but the world knew him not. This is the highest reprice in human history. (Are we repeating it today?)

In our culture, we attribute critical thinking with the intellect. When we address the topic from a Scriptural standpoint, we must bring in the heart, soul, mind and strength. With the intellect we can study the three categories of sin from 1st John along with the scriptures that teach us the results of following after those lusts; however, lust deals with the emotions. The intellect can't relate to that. Lust is a force that produces intense desire for something or someone. Your intellect can tell you something is wrong; but your lust drives you to seek fulfillment anyway. Paul teaches in Romans 7:23 about the ongoing conflict in each of us; another law at work within us that is at war with our minds. It is a raging battle and it has eternal consequences.

The enemy, Satan, wants to control all of us – every single part. And he's out to do so by appealing to our physical desires, our ego, and our urge to be our own god. The demonic nature of pride is that it does not recognize God for who He is. A proud person forgets he is the creature and God is the Creator.

The first commandment of the ten given to Moses in Exodus 20:3-17 KJV stated, "Thou shalt have no other gods before me." And in the New Testament Jesus taught us that the greatest commandment is, "Thou shalt love the Lord thy God with all thy heart, and with all thy soul, and with all thy mind." Matthew 22:37-38 KJV.

God has given humans the ability to make choices. This power of choice is stronger than the power of weapons of mass destruction, terrorists, nuclear bombs, F5 tornadoes, Category 5 hurricanes and earthquakes all together. If we are grounded in love and humility this power of choice is sobering to us. Conversely, if we are not grounded in love and humility the power to make choices is intoxicating to us. We can describe an intoxicated person as follows:

- Judgment is impaired
- Decision making is not sound
- Vision is impaired
- Reflexes are not in synch
- Speech is not clear

No one is exempt from the devices of Satan – individually or collectively. We see from reading about the seven churches of Asia in Revelation chapters

2 & 3 how collectively we can be vulnerable to the "wiles of Satan." In Revelation 2:1-7 we find the Spirit warning the church at Ephesus that unless they repented, He would come and remove their candlestick. Here was an organized group of people engaged in God's work. What can we learn from studying this passage about Ephesus?

The church at Ephesus is first addressed as being the place where John chiefly resided; and the city itself was the metropolis of that part of Asia. The positives about Ephesus:

- They bore persecution patiently
- They could not tolerate evil men
- They put fictitious apostles to the test and found them to be liars

The negative about Ephesus according to Revelation was they left their first love. In reading Revelation 2:4, it appears Satan managed to deceive this hard-working congregation. How is it possible? For the answer, we can go back to the three categories of sin taught in 1st John. Satan appeals to the appetites of humans in order to work his way in.

Ephesus had established its own identity. They had become known as the place that could spot a fictitious apostle in their midst. They were bold enough to put them on trial and prove that they were liars. No doubt they were passionate. This was appealing to the human appetite for recognition and power. Satan continued to feed that appetite.

The identity Ephesus had established now had to be promoted and protected. Ephesus became their own first love and God was moved to a lower status. Paul had admonished this congregation in his epistle years before to be renewed in the spirit of their minds (Ephesians 4:23) and to walk in love (Ephesians 5:2); however, they became lax. They started worshipping the creation more than the Creator.

Satan doesn't care how many good works an individual or a group performs or how large their following is as long as they are their "own first love" instead of God. How does the flesh get this kind of foothold in our lives and in our churches? Corruption describes a change from what is solid. When we choose to accommodate our desires, we move away from what is solid to something that isn't solid. It's like building on air. The balloon takes on the appearance of being solid until something sharp penetrates the skin of the balloon. It's then we see it was filled with air rather than a solid substance.

In Matthew chapters 5 – 7 Jesus taught us His platform – the Kingdom's value system. God gives man the choice to embrace and build with His values or we can choose our own course. When we choose our own course, we build on air and there will be a collapse at some point. Galatians 6:7 KJV, "Be not deceived; God is not mocked: for whatsoever a man soweth, that shall he also reap." Paul refers to Satan as the god of this world. "In whom the god of this world hath blinded the minds of them which believe not, lest the light of the glorious gospel of Christ, who is the image of God, should shine unto them." 2 Corinthians 4:4 KJV. He also refers to him as the prince of the power of the air, "Wherein in time past ye walked according to the course of this world, according to the prince of the power of the air, the spirit that now worketh in the children of disobedience." Ephesians 2:2 KJV

There is a battle raging between light and darkness, right and wrong, good and evil. As long as individuals, governments, institutions, churches, organizations build on God's values; directed by God's Word and His Spirit, their culture will be the same as the Kingdom culture that Jesus taught in the Sermon on the Mount (Matthew chapters 5-7). It's only when man "ascends to the throne" that the institutional culture takes on a different look from the Kingdom culture.

No place in history can we find that God's will has ultimately been dwarfed. He didn't need the approval or the cooperation of the Pharisees for His son, Jesus, to be born into this world; teach us His kingdom values, and to carry out the plan of salvation. Many prominent Jews found themselves on the outside as God's will was being performed in their day. No doubt there are multitudes of people today who have chosen their will over God's who will shortly find themselves powerless as they observe God completing His plan through people totally surrendered to Him.

King Saul's behavior demonstrated an "own first love" mentality. He held to his own agenda. He built walls of protection. He lashed out at his perceived enemies. He became convinced that the preservation of his power and the survival of his position relied solely upon himself. This explains his treatment to David. This type of treatment is acceptable in the leader's mind because he is pursuing the furtherance of his agenda. Saul enjoyed the success of David until he saw it as a threat to him. He then demoted David and watched for a reason to destroy him.

In *The Story of Jesus*, James Stalker describes the condition of the religious world that Jesus was born into. Instead of meeting a nation mature in holiness and consecrated to its heaven-ordained task, He found the first work which lay before Him was to proclaim a reformation.

> The Pharisees were the representative religious people of the time. They were champions of separateness from other nations. Emphasis was on holiness; however, they substituted rituals in place of internal wholeness. They believed they were favorites of Heaven because they were descendants of Abraham. They lost sight of the importance of personal character. They used their position for selfish gratification. They were into positional authority. Loyalty was more important to them than integrity. Image was everything. They attempted to control people. They had an inflated view of themselves. The scribes belonged to the Pharisaic Party. They were both the interpreters and copyists of the Scriptures and the lawyers of the people. They became dry ministers of the Word; though very educated. They felt their interpretation of a passage was as authoritative as the text itself. Matthew 15:2. They learned to incorporate a self-serving spin to explain away the weightiest moral obligations, and to make up for the neglect of them by increasing rituals. They were spiritually diseased within, but they covered it over with a self-deceptive religiosity on the outside. Matthew 23:27; Luke 18:10-14.

> The Sadducees were the protesters of the establishment. They cried out against ritual. They demanded a return to the true meaning of the Scripture; but their protests were self-centered rather than God-centered. They were skeptical, cold-hearted and worldly. They refused to burden their consciences with the painful demands of the Pharisees; but it was because they wished to live a life of comfort and self-indulgence.

In external appearance, it seemed progress had been made. Synagogues were multiplied. Every Sabbath they were filled with praying congregations; exhortations were delivered. The Old Testament was read once a year. Schools of theology had sprung up.

In spite of all this religious behavior, spirituality had sadly declined. The externals had been multiplied, but the inner spirit was starved.

"Woe unto you, scribes and Pharisees, hypocrites! For ye pay tithe of mint and anise and cumin, and have omitted the weightier matters of the law, judgment, mercy, and faith: these ought ye to have done, and not to leave the other undone. Ye blind guides, which strain at a gnat, and swallow a camel. Woe unto you, scribes and Pharisees, hypocrites for ye make clean the outside of the cup and of the platter, but within they are full of extortion and excess." Matthew 23:23-25 KJV. "Woe to you, scribes and Pharisees, hypocrites! For ye are like unto whited sepulchers, which indeed appear beautiful outward, but are within full of dead men's bones, and of all uncleanness." Matthew 23:27 KJV.

When Christ is the center, He directs the mission according to His will. Paul kept himself in check and said, "I preach Christ and Him crucified." He didn't preach Paul's plan. That took the results out of his hands and put them into God's hands. That kept wholeness in his message and kept corruption out. "Unless the Lord builds the house, those who build it labor in vain." Psalm 127:1a ESV.

An excerpt from Billy Murray's sermon titled, Thy Kingdom Come (1987):

The religious institution into which Jesus was born was not lacking in form. The machinery of institutional government was in place. They had their prescribed forms of worship which they carried out meticulously; they had the written Word to which they gave much lip service with a great show of piety. They thought they knew the Scriptures; they could have quoted them at length, but they were ignorant of the substance, the life, the power, the inspiration of God's Holy Word. When the Word was made flesh and dwelt among them, they could not identify Him with the Scriptures they professed to know. Many remained blind and insensitive to His presence.

Even as the kingdom then was suffering violence, or upheaval, so now there is a battle raging. It is a battle between the Spirit and the flesh, and at times the lines of demarcation seem blurred. But these lines will become clearer, and those who are determined that the church is going to be a spiritual house, operating with kingdom power, will be forceful in pressing into a new dimension of kingdom living."

Chapter 4
Whose Own Strength is Their God

Habakkuk 1:1-11 – the prophecy that Habakkuk the prophet received.

Frank M. Boyd writes:

> This prophecy was given on the eve of Judah's captivity to Babylon, as the "great day of the Lord," spoken of by Zephaniah, was about to break. Assyria, a great world power, was fading fast under the blows of the rising Babylonian might. The Babylonian power was sweeping westward like a flood (1:5-11), but had not yet reached Judah (3:16).

> Habakkuk may have been saddened by the tragic death of good King Josiah, at Megiddo, where he engaged in a vain attempt to frustrate the plans of Pharaoh-Necho of Egypt (2 Chronicles 35:20-34).

> Mighty upheavals were taking place in world history. Habakkuk was in the midst of them, felt their impact, and was greatly perplexed.

> It is said that Benjamin Franklin read Habakkuk to a literary circle in Paris, winning their unanimous tribute of admiration for an author of whom not one of them had ever heard before.

> The book may have been a favorite with Paul. He quotes 1:5 in his warning to the unbelieving Jews at Antioch (Acts 13:41), and the famous statement of 2:4 he quotes three times (Romans 1:17; Galatians 3:11; Hebrews 10:38).

Two-thirds of Habakkuk is conversational or dialogue between the prophet and the Lord.

Habakkuk's Complaint (verses 2-4 NIV)

"How long, Lord, must I call for help, but You do not listen? Or cry out to You, "Violence!" but You do not save? Why do You make me look at injustice? Why do You tolerate wrongdoing? Destruction and violence are before me; there is strife, and conflict abounds. Therefore, the law is paralyzed, and justice never prevails. The wicked hem in the righteous, so that justice is perverted."

Habakkuk was a man with deep perplexities. He has been called the "freethinker among the prophets," but he was a man of clear faith and powerful hold upon God. He was a man of reverent spirit, with keen, sensitive, highly developed faculties, but he was more seriously troubled than any other man in the kingdom.

Habakkuk was undoubtedly familiar with the words and works of Amos, Hosea, Micah, and Isaiah. He knew the precepts and promises of the Law of Moses. He was a careful student of life and experience of men.

Habakkuk is perplexed with the silence and forbearance of God permitting evil to continue and pours out his soul to God. He is perplexed over 1) the seeming neglect of his prayer; 2) at the Lord's seeming indifference to sin and suffering. Why, he asks, does God allow the wicked and lawless men of Judah to continue unpunished? How long will God allow the injustice, the brutality, the wrong to go on in Jerusalem?

The Lord's Answer (verses 5-11 NIV)

"Look at the nations and watch – and be utterly amazed, for I am going to do something in your days that you would not believe, even if you were told. I am raising up the Babylonians, that ruthless and impetuous people, who sweep across the whole earth to seize dwellings not their own. They are a feared and dreaded people; they are a law to themselves and promote their own honor. Their horses are swifter than leopards, fiercer than wolves at dusk. Their cavalry gallops headlong; their horsemen come from afar. They fly like an eagle swooping to devour; they all come intent on violence. Their hordes advance like the desert wind and gather prisoners like sand. They mock kings and scoff at rulers. They laugh at all fortified cities; by building earthen ramps they capture them. Then they sweep past like the wind and go on – guilty people, whose own strength is their god."

God answers by stating that His silence does not mean ignorance nor indifference. He is not inattentive nor inactive, but He is about to bring punishment upon sinful Judah. God's reply challenges Habakkuk to look beyond the limited borders of Judah. God's reply revealed that He is:

1. About to do something incredible (v 5)
2. Will use these Chaldeans to chastise Judah for its sin (v 6)
3. Has chosen them as terrible and dreadful instruments who will cause an awful scourge to sweep over the land. Judgment will come upon Judah.

The last part of verse 11, "guilty people, whose own strength is their god" makes us cringe. We explain it away by saying this is a statement about wicked heathens. Much like the king's response in Daniel 4:30, "and the king answered and said, 'Is not this great Babylon, which I have built by my mighty power as a royal residence and for the glory of my majesty?'" Or, Ezekiel 28:2, "Son of man, say to the prince of Tyre, Thus says the Lord God: 'Because your heart is proud, and you have said, I am a god, I sit in the seat of the gods, in the heart of the seas,' yet you are but a man, and no god, though you make your heart like the heart of a god." Paul writes in 2 Thessalonians 2:4 ESV, "...who opposes and exalts himself against every so-called god or object of worship, so that he takes his seat in the temple of God, proclaiming himself to be God."

This is ALL pride. It ceases to think of itself as God's instrument, and so becomes a god itself, as though its eminence and strength were its own, and its wisdom were the source of its power and its will the measure of greatness.

Yes, these verses describing such pride have the same effect on us as nails across a chalk board. But then our ears are crushed to study

Jeremiah 2:13, where God was speaking through His prophet about His own people:

> When Israel became confused and disoriented about who God was and who they were, it produced desolate, empty, broken down cities. "The city of confusion is broken down." Isaiah 24:10 KJV. This passage is describing a deserted, worthless thing, an empty place, vanity, waste, and wilderness. Nehemiah prayed over the broken-down walls and burned gates of Jerusalem. "God, we have treated You like dirt." Nehemiah 1:7 MSG. God spoke through Jeremiah, "My people have committed two sins: they have forsaken Me, the spring of living water, and have dug their own cisterns, broken cisterns, that cannot hold water." Jeremiah 2:13 NIV.

Pride keeps us from dealing with the truth. It distorts our vision. It hardens our hearts and dims our eyes of understanding. Jeremiah 3:25 KJV, "Our confusion covereth us." It takes repentance to set us free. Paul said in 2 Timothy 2:25-26 KJV, "If God peradventure will give them repentance to the acknowledging of the truth; and that they may recover themselves out of the snare of the devil, who are taken captive by him at his will."

God doesn't compromise His Kingdom values by anointing the superficial (empty air). Anytime we become our "own first love", we defeat ourselves. Satan doesn't even have to devise a plan against us. We defeat ourselves. Are we enough of a threat to Satan for him to devise a plan against us?

"For this people's heart is waxed gross, and their ears are dull of hearing, and their eyes they have closed; lest at any time they should see with their eyes, and hear with their ears, and should understand with their heart, and should be converted, and I should heal them." Matthew 13:15 KJV.

Deuteronomy 30:15-16 KJV, "See, I have set before thee this day life and good, death and evil, in that I command thee this day to love the Lord thy God, to walk in His ways, and to keep His commandments and His statutes and His judgments, that thou mayest live and multiply: and the Lord thy God shall bless thee in the land whither thou goest to possess it." The Lord is calling and anointing people in the 21st Century who are not confused about who they are and who God is. Isaiah 59:20 NIV, "'The Redeemer will come to Zion, to those in Jacob who repent of their sins,' declares the Lord."

"If My people, which are called by My name, shall humble themselves, and pray, and seek My face, and turn from their wicked ways; then will I hear from heaven, and will forgive their sin, and will heal their land." 2 Chronicles 7:14 KJV.

Chapter 5

Lord, Test Our Motives

L ord, test our motives. It seems like it is so easy for us to violate Your principles in order to accomplish our goals. We decide what we want to do and then we create a reason for doing it.

GotQuestions.org writes the following concerning motives:

> A motive is the underlying reason for any action. Proverbs 16:2 says, "All a person's ways seem pure to them, but motives are weighed by the Lord." Because the human heart is very deceitful (Jeremiah 17:9), we can easily fool ourselves about our own motives. We can pretend that we are choosing certain actions for God or the benefit of others, when in reality we have selfish reasons. God is not fooled by our selfishness and is "a discerner of the thoughts and intents of the heart." Hebrews 4:12 KJV.

> Human beings can operate from a variety of motivations: pride, anger, revenge, a sense of entitlement, or the desire for approval can all be catalysts for our actions. Selfish motives can hinder our prayers. James 4:3 NIV, "When you ask, you do not receive, because you ask with wrong motives, that you may spend what you get on your pleasures." Because our hearts are so deceitful. We should constantly evaluate our own motives and be willing to be honest with ourselves about why we are choosing a certain action.

> We can even minister from impure motives (Philippians 1:17), but God is not impressed (Proverbs 21:27). Jesus spoke to this

issue in Matthew 6:1 NIV when He said, "Be careful not to practice your righteousness in front of others to be seen by them. If you do, you will have no reward from your Father in heaven."

What is the right motivation? Thessalonians 2:4 NLT, "Our purpose is to please God, not people. He alone examines the motives of our hearts." God is interested in our motives even more than our actions. 1 Corinthians 4:5 states that when Jesus comes again, He will bring to light what is hidden in darkness and will expose the motives of the heart. He knows why we do what we do. We can keep our motives pure by continually surrendering every part of our hearts to His Holy Spirit.

A list of questions to help us evaluate our own motives:

- If no one ever knows what I am doing (giving, serving, sacrificing), would I still do it?
- If there was no visible payoff for doing this, would I still do it?
- Would I joyfully take a lesser role if God asked me to?
- Am I doing this for the praise of others or how it makes me feel?
- If I had to suffer for continuing what God has called me to do, would I continue?
- If others misunderstand or criticize my actions, will I stop?
- If those whom I am serving never show gratitude or repay me in any way, will I still do it?
- Do I judge my success or failure based upon my faithfulness to what God has asked me to do or how I compare with others?

Conclusion
Standing in the Valley of Decision

We are standing in the valley of decision gazing at the greater things of God, the culmination of all things, set before us. As we get a glimpse of the splendor of God's glory, it seems that making the decision to move forward should be an easy one. However, upon closer observation, we find that we are engaged in a life-or-death battle with self.

If we choose to move forward it means that we have made a commitment to lay down our individual plans and to pick up unity of purpose that only comes from submitting to God. It means that we are cleansing ourselves of all selfish motives allowing our actions to be fueled only by the love of God. It means that we are striving to mature from self-centeredness to God-centeredness. It means we are aligning our message and actions with those of Christ. It means we are moving from self-reliance to working together. It means teamwork, cooperation, and communication, all of which are enemies of self-centeredness; but are allies of the greater whole.

In his book, *Fearfully & Wonderfully Made*, Dr. Paul Brand states:

Following Christ involves self-denial, including pain. We are called to self-denial, not for its own sake, but for the compensation that we can obtain in no other way. Today's culture exalts self-fulfillment, self-discovery, and autonomy. But according to Christ, it is only in losing my life that I will find it. Only by committing

31

myself as a "living sacrifice" to the larger Body through loyalty to Him will I find my true reason for being.

Christ taught us in His Sermon on the Mount, God's principles for living in the form of a few simple truths summarized in *The Leadership Wisdom of Jesus,* Charles C. Manz:

- The key to being first is being last
- The key to living is dying
- The key to being free is being Christ's slave
- The key to getting is giving
- The key to being a leader is being a servant
- The key to being exalted is to live a life of humility

Humility is what determines one's status in the Kingdom of God.

How will history record our decision?

<u>List of Resources:</u>

Scripture quotations from the English Standard Version (ESV), The Authorized (King James) Version (KJV), the New International Version (NIV), New American Standard Bible (NASB), and New Living Translation (NLT).

Critical Thinking X504, Fall 2000, Professor Michael B. Metzger; Kelley School of Business, Indiana University

The Leadership Wisdom of Jesus, Charles C. Manz, Berrett-Koehler Publishers, Inc. San Francisco, 1998

While Men Sleep, Janice Miller, 2016, CreateSpace Independent Publishing Platform, North Charleston, SC

Fearfully & Wonderfully Made, Dr. Paul Brand & Philip Yancey, Zondervan Books, Zondervan Publishing House, Grand Rapids, Michigan, 1980

Old Testament, Frank M. Boyd, Berean School of the Bible, Springfield, MO

Gotquestions.org

The FoundationforCriticalThinking.org

www.ingramcontent.com/pod-product-compliance
Lightning Source LLC
Chambersburg PA
CBHW051601120626
46551CB00013B/1624